Nelson

ENGLISH

SKILLS

BOOK 2

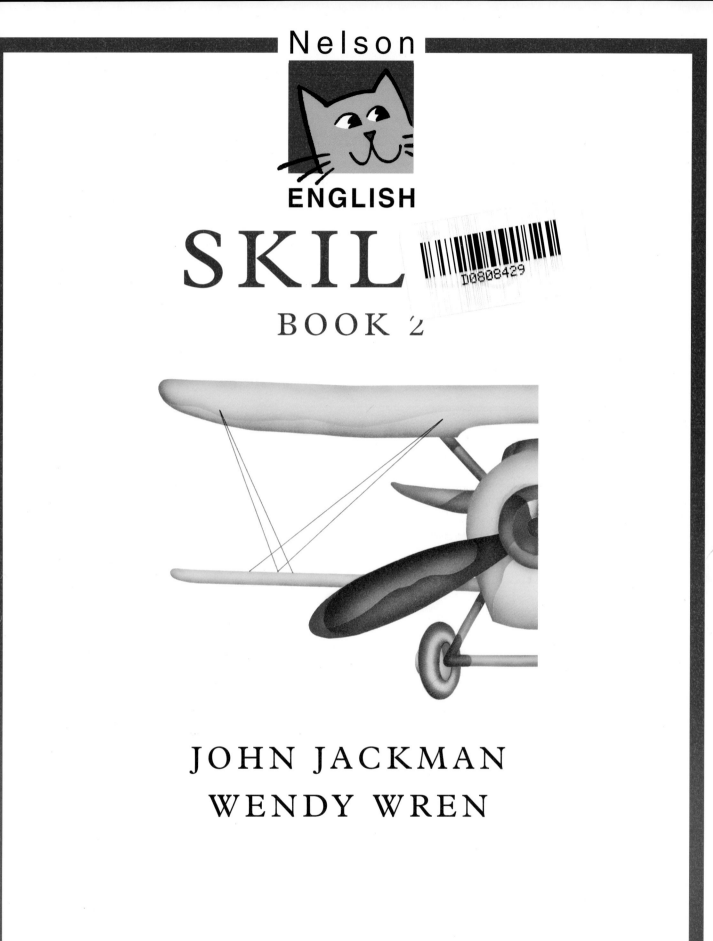

JOHN JACKMAN
WENDY WREN

Nelson

Contents

Vocabulary	Punctuation/ Grammar	Spelling	Quiz
there/their dictionary work	punctuation marks	or	Parthenon challenge (making words)
dictionary work collective nouns	punctuation marks	sh ch	What am I? (word riddle)
right/write	direct speech inverted commas	adding 'ing'	Code cracker (letter codes)
classification antonyms	direct speech verbs	ai ay	punctuation puzzle
dictionary definitions	direct speech adverbs	ew	word families
numbers and colours	comparatives and superlatives, adverbs	oa	Bridge builders (word puzzle)
words and pictures compound words	proper nouns	plurals, ('s', 'x', 'ch', 'sh' endings)	dictionary guide words
compound words similes, word families	active verbs being verbs	oy, oi plurals ('y' endings)	optical illusion
dictionary definitions contractions	paragraphs punctuation marks	aw	missing vowels
questions	possessive nouns	igh silent 'k'	vowel wordsquares
bought/brought	subjects and verbs	ea	Royal riddle (word riddle)
gender words	punctuation marks	ough	odd-one-out
synonyms	direct speech, subjects and predicates	'o' sound	
abbreviations	suffix	er, ir, ur	About yourself (phrases)

The glory of Athens

Athens is a city in Greece. About 2000 years ago the people there worshipped the goddess of wisdom called Athena. They wanted to please Athena, so they built temples for her on a hill in the centre of their city. This area was called the Acropolis, which means 'high city'. The grandest temple on the Acropolis was the Parthenon. Many of its columns still stand today.

Most people did not go inside the Parthenon as people go into churches, temples or mosques today. They prayed outside. Inside was simply a huge statue of Athena made from gold and ivory.

The Acropolis was also a place for everyone to meet and enjoy themselves. There were many festivals and people would come in their best clothes. Sometimes there were sacrifices, which meant everyone had free meat to eat. This was a luxury because there was little space for people to keep farm animals in Athens.

Glossary
a *glossary* explains what a word means
sacrifice means killing an animal for a god
luxury means expensive and enjoyable

COMPREHENSION

A Copy these sentences. Fill in the missing words.

1 The hill in the centre of Athens was called the ____.

2 The people built ____ for the goddess Athena.

3 The grandest temple was the ____.

B Write a sentence to answer each question.

1 What was inside the Parthenon?

2 What was the Parthenon built for?

3 Why was it unusual for the people to eat meat in Athens?

VOCABULARY

there and their

> **There** usually means a place.
> To help you remember, look for the smaller word 'here' in **there**. 'Here' also means a place.
> *Example:* The temple is over **there**.
> **Their** means 'belonging to them'. It is about people. In the middle of their is 'i(I)' which is also to do with people.
> *Example:* The Greeks were proud of **their** temples.

A Is **there** or **their** missing from these sentences?

1 ____ were many beautiful temples in Athens.

2 The people built temples to please ____ goddess Athena.

3 ____ were many festivals.

4 "We like to go ____ with our parents," said the children.

5 One of ____ friends competed in the Olympic Games.

6 You can still see some remains of the Parthenon ____.

The words in your dictionary are in alphabetical order.
Words which begin with a come first,
next are b words, then c words,
and so on until the z words, which are last.

abcdefghijklmnopqrstuvwxyz

A Sort these words into alphabetical order.

   1 Greece, Acropolis, Parthenon

   2 sacrifice, animals, temple

   3 festival, ivory, gold, statue, columns

There are lots of words which begin with the same letter.
Dictionaries would be very difficult to use if the words
were all jumbled together, so we need to look at the next
letters as well. The following words have been sorted by
looking at the second letters:
about, acorn, add, aeroplane, after.

B Sort these groups of words into alphabetical order.
You will need to look at the second letters.

   1 actor, able, aeroplane, adder, afraid

   2 Athens, Acropolis, Alos, Andros

   3 drama, dancers, discus, Delphi

   4 myth, metal, marble, mosaic

PUNCTUATION

Capital letters
Full stops
Question marks
Commas

> We always begin a sentence with a **capital letter**. We usually end it with a **full stop** (.) or **question mark** (?). We use a **comma** (,) to separate each word in a list.
> *Example:* The Greeks had many different gods including Athena, Zeus, Bacchus, Poseidon and Dionysus.

A Write these sentences correctly.

1 the games were held in honour of Zeus

2 the first games were for men only

3 wrestling jumping archery and javelin were main events

4 an olive branch was given to each of the winners

5 today men and women can take part

6 would you like to go to the Olympic Games

SPELLING

'or' pattern

A Play the game by bouncing around the square.
One word is done for you: c + **or** + k = c**or**k

c	h	th	f	h
st				w
m		**or**		ch
p				se
n	k	sh	t	y

1 Start in a small square. Write the letter down.

2 Bounce into the middle and write **or**.

3 Then bounce into another square to get the last letter.

How many **or** words can you collect?

QUIZ

Parthenon challenge

There are nine letters in the word **Parthenon**.
How many words can you make using some or all of these letters? Use a dictionary to help you check the spellings.

7

On a sheep farm

Most sheep farms in Britain are in the hills of Scotland, Wales and the north and west of England. Flocks graze on the steep hillsides.

Sheep in the hills do not move far so farmers can usually find their flocks, but most sheep are marked just in case they stray.

Spring is a busy time when the lambs are born. The shepherds hope for good weather so that they can reach the ewes and lambs. New lambs may die if they get wet and cold.

In the summer the lambs are dipped and given injections to stop them catching illnesses. The sheep are sheared and the wool is sold to factories to make cloth.

After three or four months most of the young sheep are sent to market, but some are kept for breeding next year's lambs.

Glossary

flock means a group of sheep
graze means eat grass
ewe means a female sheep
ram means a male sheep

COMPREHENSION

A Copy these sentences. Fill in the missing words.

1 Sheep graze on the steep ____.

2 The ewes give birth to the ____ in Spring.

3 If the new lambs get ____ and ____ they may die.

B Write a sentence to answer each question.

1 Where are most of the sheep farms in Britain?

2 Why does the farmer not usually lose the sheep?

3 Why are the sheep dipped and given injections?

VOCABULARY

Dictionary work

Remember, we sort words into alphabetical order by looking at the **first** letter. If we have more than one word with the same first letter, we put these in order by looking at the **second** letter.

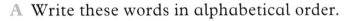

A Write these words in alphabetical order.

1 little, leaf, lamb

2 sheep, safe, Scotland

3 weather, wool, white, Wales

4 ewe, England, escape, eat

B Now write these words in the order they appear in a dictionary.

1 grain, goat, house, hill

2 sheep, ox, hare, horse, owl

3 barn, high, hay, dip, bucket

C Look up these words in your dictionary.
Write the meaning, or definition, of each one.

1 animal   2 adder   3 alike   4 ascend

Collective nouns

flock

herd

A **noun** is a name of a person, place or thing.
A **collective noun** is a special name of a collection of people, places or things.

A Copy these lists. Draw lines to link them.

noun	collective noun
sailors	team
books	crowd
people	forest
players	crew
trees	library

B Choose a collective noun from the box for each noun.
Write your answer in a short sentence.
Like this: 1 The flock of sheep was on the hill.

1 sheep	2 cows	3 kittens
4 flowers	5 bees	6 dogs

herd	swarm	pack	flock	bunch	litter

PUNCTUATION

Punctuation marks

A All the capital letters and punctuation marks have been left out of these sentences. Write them correctly.

1 a male sheep is called a ram

2 the lambs are born in the spring

3 some lambs have to be cared for by the farmer

B Now write these sentences putting in the capital letters and punctuation marks.

can you see the sheep high on the hills the farmer has a large flock his sheep dogs are called betsy nan bob and dex one of the ewes has two lambs the farmer is looking after them in a field near the farm last spring he let me feed some of the lambs from a bottle i hope he ll let me do it again this year

C Write two sentences about each picture. Don't forget the capital letters and full stops.

SPELLING

'sh' and 'ch' patterns

A Draw a large picture of a sheep on your page.
Find as many **sh** words as you can to write on the sheep.

B The word 'church' begins and ends with **ch**. Find three words that begin with **ch**, and three that end with **ch**, to finish this puzzle. Use a dictionary if you need to.

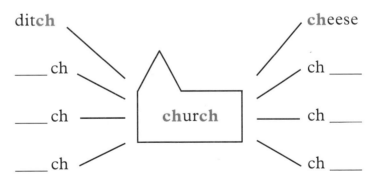

QUIZ

What am I?

Try to solve this riddle.

My first letter is in 'let' but not in 'get'.
My second letter is in 'gave' but not in 'give'.
My third letter is in 'mat' but not in 'hat'.
My last letter is in 'big' but not in 'wig'.
What am I?

Now write a riddle of your own. Try it on a friend.

Today I ate . . .

. . . a bowl of cereal, two slices of
toast and a glass of orange,
a bag of crisps and some milk,
a burger with chips and an apple,
a bag of sweets,
sausages with beans and potatoes,
rice pudding and jam,
and a cup of cocoa and
some biscuits.

. . . a special biscuit, a bowl of
broth, and two cups of water . . .
and yesterday I had nothing.

Most of us are lucky – we get food every day. Over
half the people in the world are not so lucky. Many
people have to go several days without any food. Their
bodies use up the fat and they become thin.
They feel weak and tired.

Many people cannot earn money to buy food
and are too weak or ill to grow it themselves. In
some countries they cannot grow food because
there is not enough rain or because there is a war.

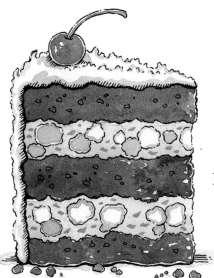

COMPREHENSION

A Copy these sentences. Fill in the missing words.

1 Over ____ the people in the world do not have enough to eat.

2 If people don't have enough food their bodies become ____.

3 This makes them feel ____ and ____.

B Write a sentence to answer each question.

1 What is your favourite food?

2 Who buys your food?

3 Why do some people find it difficult to get food?

VOCABULARY

right and write

Right means several things, such as:

– the opposite of wrong.
Example: It is **right** to help hungry children.

– the opposite of left.
Example: Look **right** and left when crossing the road.

– all the way.
Example: The bus went **right** to the centre.

Write means to use letters or signs, usually on a piece of paper.

A Choose **right** or **write** to finish these sentences.

1 It is not ____ that many people are hungry.

2 Our school will ____ to Oxfam and send them the money we raised this year.

3 The girl slipped ____ over and hurt her leg.

4 Cakes are on the left and bread is on the ____.

5 ____ neatly so that he can read your letter.

6 Is it ____ to show starving people on television?

Direct speech
Inverted commas

Sometimes inverted commas are called 'speech marks'.

Sometimes we need to write the words that someone has spoken. This is called **direct speech**.

Direct speech should begin and end with **inverted commas** (" "). Inverted commas tell us when people have started to say something, and when they have finished. *Example:* Naomi said, "I like sweets."

A Copy the words that the person said in each sentence.

1 The farmer said, "My crops won't grow because it hasn't rained for months."

2 Amrit said, "I like custard with my pudding."

3 Mrs Timms said, "Our school concert this year is in aid of Save the Children."

B Copy these sentences. Put inverted commas round the words that the person actually said.

1 James said, I like sweets.

2 Shall we have a picnic? asked Ruth.

3 Gill said, I like chips.

4 Would you like some fruit? said Gran.

SPELLING

Adding 'ing'

Remember, the vowels are a, e, i, o, u.

When you add **ing** to a very short word, look at the letter before the last letter. Is it a single vowel (a, e, i, o, u)?
If it is, double the last letter. Then add **ing**.
If it isn't, just add **ing**.
Examples:

b**a**t, bat**ting**   sh**o**p, shop**ping**

s**i**ng, sing**ing**   r**ea**d, read**ing**

This doesn't work for words ending in **w**, **x** or **y**.

A Add **ing** to these short words.

1 win	2 sit	3 hit	4 pat
5 get	6 slip	7 miss	8 spell
9 start	10 ask	11 wish	12 push

B Add **ing** to these short words. Some of the words end in **w**, **x** or **y**, so you just need to add **ing**.

1 box	2 fit	3 sow	4 try
5 mow	6 grow	7 fly	8 hiss

QUIZ

Code cracker

Look at this code. If you want to send a secret message you can use a code like this.

```
a b c d e f g h i j k l m n o p q r s t u v w x y z
      ▼       ▼                             ▼
z a b c d e f g h i j k l m n o p q r s t u v w x y
```

1 First write your message on a piece of paper.

2 Then check the code table to find the code letter to use in place of each normal letter. Like this:

I went to the shop
H vd

Instead of **I** write **H** , instead of **w** write **v** , instead of **e** write **d** , and so on.

Finish this message.
Make up another message in code to send to your friend.

Viking ships

The Vikings came across the North Sea to the British Isles from Norway, Sweden and Denmark. In those days many people were afraid of the sea, but the Vikings had made ships which were able to sail across rough seas safely.

The Viking warships, called 'longships', were wide and flat-bottomed so that they could sail close to the beaches, and had a large sail which meant that they could travel very quickly. As the compass had not been invented, the Vikings navigated by looking at the stars or sun. When the ships were in battle, they would have a dragon head fixed to the front of the boat, or the prow. This was taken off in port because the sailors thought it brought bad luck.

The Vikings became bolder as their ships became faster. They sailed up the River Thames and attacked London. They also sailed along the River Seine in France to attack Paris.

As well as longships, the Vikings had 'traders' and 'ferries'. We know this from the remains of vessels found buried in the mud.

COMPREHENSION

A Copy these sentences. Fill in the missing words.

1 Viking ships had a large ____.

2 A ____ ____ was fixed to the prow.

3 The other name for a Viking warship was a ____.

B Write a sentence to answer each question.

1 Why was the dragon's head sometimes removed?

2 How do we know so much about Viking ships?

3 Why might Viking sailors have found it difficult to find their way at sea on a cloudy night?

VOCABULARY

Classification

Classifying is sorting things into groups.
Example: Vikings, Saxons, Romans = **invaders**

A What is the classification name of each of these?

1 longship, trader, ferry =

2 potato, carrot, cabbage =

3 Thames, Seine, Clyde =

4 brown, green, blue =

5 Paris, London, York =

B Copy these three headings.

made of metal   **made of wood**   **made of plastic**

Classify some of the objects in your classroom under each heading. Some objects may go under more than one heading.

Antonyms

Antonyms are words with opposite meanings.
Examples: thick, thin   wet, dry

A Which word in brackets is the antonym of these words?

1 rough (cold, smooth, heavy, hard)

2 large (dirty, full, big, small)

3 wide (narrow, fat, round, large)

4 fast (quick, speed, slow, follow)

Now write the words in sentences to show what they mean.

B Write **un** in front of these words.

| 1 dress | 2 tie | 3 fold | 4 well |
| 5 load | 6 pack | 7 employed | 8 true |

What happens to the meaning of the word? Write four of these new words in sentences to show what each means.

PUNCTUATION

Direct speech

Remember, we put **inverted commas** or speech marks (" ") at the beginning and end of the words people say.

The commas give you a clue.

A Copy these sentences and add the inverted commas.

1 The Viking leader said, We are going to set up camp in the Shetland Islands.

2 It will take us a week to get there, said the captain.

3 It is too rough to sail in this weather, said the sailors.

4 Be brave and trust me, said the captain.

It is too rough to sail in this weather.

A **verb** is an active or 'doing' word.
It tells us what is being done in a sentence.
Example: The Vikings **sail** the ship.

A Copy these word webs. Find verbs in the box which go with the nouns. Four verbs have been done for you.

trickles	paddles	ploughs	sows
sails	blazes	plants	drips
sprinkles	rows	smoulders	floods
harvests	navigates	sparks	burns

1 trickles
\ /
water
/ \

2 ploughs
\ /
farmer
/ \

3 rows
\ /
sailor
/ \

4 burns
\ /
fire
/ \

A Draw a picture which has as many **ai** and **ay** words in it as possible. Label the picture. Use a dictionary to help you.

B

1   2   3   4

Write the missing **ai** and **ay** words.

Add spaces, capital letters and full stops to these sentences.

1 thevikingscametobritainintheirlongships

2 theywerenotafraidofthesea

3 somepeopleinbritainarerelatedtothevikings

19

Viking expedition

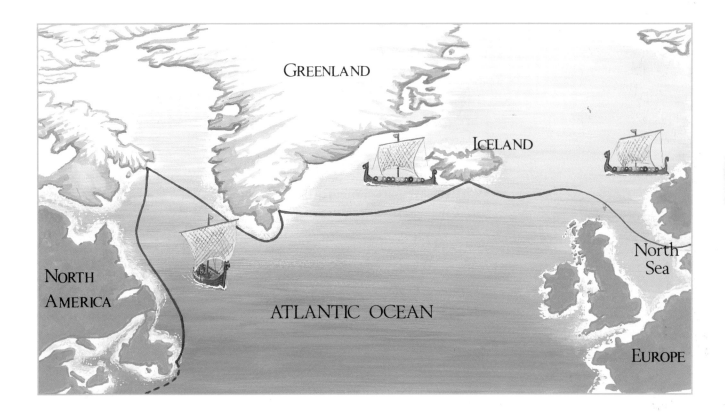

GREENLAND

ICELAND

NORTH AMERICA

ATLANTIC OCEAN

North Sea

EUROPE

Viking sailors are thought to have been the first to discover Iceland, and some Viking families decided to stay there. Other sailors, like Eric the Red, sailed further west and found Greenland. Eric's son, Leif Ericsson, sailed on even further to a place that he called Vinland. Many people think that this was America. If so, this means that the Vikings reached America nearly 500 years before Christopher Columbus.

A Viking expedition looked like a camping expedition today. They took tents and all the things they needed to survive when they first arrived. They had barrels full of salted meat and fish, and carried water and wine in leather skin bags. Soon they built houses, and villages and towns grew up. They began to trade with the local people, selling them skins, grain, cloth and slaves. They bought silk, glass, wine and, most important, metal to make their weapons.

COMPREHENSION

A Copy these sentences. Fill in the missing words.

   1 Eric the Red reached ____ .

   2 Eric's son was called ____ ____ .

   3 The Vikings took ____ to live in when they landed.

B Write a sentence to answer each question.

   1 What did Viking explorers carry with them?

   2 How did the Viking invaders change a place when they settled there?

   3 Who reached America nearly 500 years after the Vikings?

VOCABULARY

Dictionary definitions

A dictionary is very useful for checking spellings.
It also gives the meanings or **definitions** of words.

This is an entry in a dictionary:

         noun   *definition*   *example*
         ▾   ▾   ▾
exhibition *n* a display: *an art exhibition.*

Here are some more entries on the same page:

    adjective *definition*   *other words in the 'family'*
        ▾   ▾   ▾
expensive *adj* costing a lot. *opp* **inexpensive**.

      verb   *definition*
       ▾   ▾
explain *v* to make the meaning of something clear.
  explaining, explained. ◄ *other words in the 'family'*

A Find these words in your dictionary. Write their definitions and say whether they are nouns, verbs or adjectives.

   1 expert   2 explore   3 expedition   4 extraordinary

B Write your own sentences using the words **explore** and **expedition**.

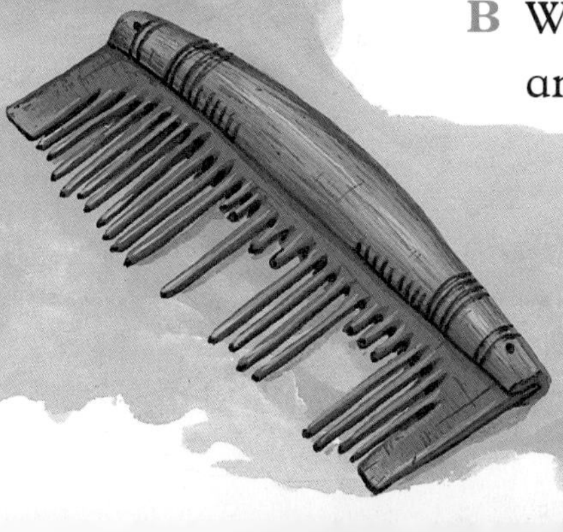

Inverted commas or speech marks (" ") tell us when people are talking. *Example:* Leif said, **"Let's land here."**

The words inside the inverted commas are treated as a smaller sentence inside a bigger sentence. These words start with a **capital letter** and end with a **full stop** or **question mark**.

However, sometimes the words that are said come first. In this case the words have a **comma**, instead of a full stop, at the end. *Example:* **"Let's land here,"** said Leif.

A Write these sentences.
Add the commas, inverted commas and capital letters.

1 Harold said I'm getting tired.

2 Olaf asked how much further do we have to go?

3 I think I can see land said Ingrid.

4 Where? said Harold excitedly.

5 Keep rowing and we'll land before dark said Leif encouragingly.

GRAMMAR

Adverbs

An **ad**verb **adds** to the verb.

An **adverb** tells us more about *how*, *when*, or *where* the action of a verb took place.
Example: said Harold
         said Harold **excitedly**
The **adverb** 'excitedly' describes how Harold spoke.
Many *how* adverbs end in **ly**.

A Copy these sentences. Underline the verbs and circle the adverbs. The adverbs tell us *how* the action took place.

1 The Vikings fought fiercely.

2 They ran quickly.

3 Their dogs barked loudly.

4 The children ate hungrily.

It's easy if you ask, "Which word tells me *when* or *where*?"

B Copy these sentences.
Underline the verbs and circle the adverbs.
The adverbs show *when* or *where* the action took place.

1 They often sailed their ships.

2 Build the fire here.

3 Light it now.

4 Always wear the lucky ring.

5 Come home soon.

C Write five sentences with adverbs in them.
Underline the verbs and circle the adverbs.

SPELLING

'ew' pattern

Limericks are short, funny rhymes with five lines.
Can you see which lines rhyme with each other?

There was an old Viking I kn**ew**
Who loved his cabbages and st**ew**.
So when they ran out
He gave a great shout
And cried, "What else can I ch**ew**?"

A Finish this limerick with **ew** rhyming words. Your limerick should have five lines. The first, second and fifth lines should rhyme with each other, and the third and fourth lines should rhyme. The words in the box may help.

There was an old man I ____
Who . . .

| stew | few | yew | knew | dew | chew | nephew |
| grew | drew | new | threw | flew | blew | view |

QUIZ

Word families

The words in these lists have something in common.
Which word in the brackets is part of each 'family'?

1 boat, ship, ferry (fish, swan, canoe, sailor)

2 Viking, Roman, Saxon (York, woman, Greek, soldier)

23

Check-up 1

A Choose one of the words in brackets to fill in the gaps.

1 ____ will be games at my party. (there, their)

2 They left ____ muddy boots outside. (there, their)

3 The ball landed over ____. (there, their)

4 I always try to ____ neatly. (write, right)

5 Turn ____ at the end of the road. (write, right)

6 She always thinks he is ____. (write, right)

B Write the collective noun for each of these.

1 sheep = flock   2 cows   3 trees

4 wolves   5 soldiers   6 books

C What is the classification of these groups?

1 potatoes, sprouts, carrots = vegetables

2 pink, blue, yellow

3 Cardiff, Belfast, Edinburgh, London

4 monkey, elephant, zebra, lion

D Which word in the brackets is the antonym?

1 large (under, small, in, dirty) = small

2 smooth (heavy, slippery, rough, gentle)

3 slow (runner, fast, old, big)

4 inside (on, over, outside, top)

E Find these words in a dictionary. Write their definitions.

1 earl   2 tint   3 Passover   4 artificial

24

A Add capital letters, full stops and question marks to
the sentences.

1 i like my kitten   2 she is black and white

3 her name is sally   4 do you have a pet

B Add capital letters, commas, question marks and full stops
to the sentences.

1 can i have a birthday party

2 we will need to buy some cakes biscuits crisps and pizza

3 can peter anna ali kim and sam come to my party

C Add inverted commas (speech marks) to the sentences.

1 That was a really brilliant party, said Ali.

2 Thanks for inviting us, added Peter and Anna.

3 Sam said, will you come to my party next week?

D A verb is an 'active' word. Adverbs tell us *how*, *when* or
where the action is happening. Underline the verbs and
circle the adverbs.

1 The children ran home quickly.

2 The cat purred gently.

3 I fell heavily and hurt my knee.

4 Cross the road here.

5 "You always win," said Tina.

A Add **ing** to these. You may need to double the last letter.

1 jump   2 get   3 put   4 wish

5 push   6 sit   7 pat   8 fall

B Put these words in alphabetical order.

1 Tom, Amy, Stewart, Yin   2 cup, chair, car, clock

3 apple, bath, dog, actor   4 were, word, wise, Wales

Bridges

People have built bridges for thousands of years. The first were very simple, like a log or a large slab of stone across a stream.

Many of the longest, modern road bridges over rivers are suspension bridges. They are made from steel cables. Two large towers are built and the steel cables are hung between them. More cables hang down from the main cables and these 'suspend' the road. This is why these bridges are called 'suspension' bridges. The road is high enough for boats to pass underneath.

Tacoma Narrows
Bridge

Engineers need to be very careful. If the design of the suspension bridge is not exactly right, it can start to twist and turn in a high wind. This happened to the Tacoma Narrows Bridge in the USA, which shook itself to pieces.

The Forth, Severn and Humber Bridges are examples of suspension bridges in Britain. The Humber Bridge has one of the longest spans in the world. Its main span is 1410 metres across.

A Copy these sentences. Fill in the missing words.

1 The simplest bridge is a ____ or a slab of stone.

2 On a suspension bridge the cables are made of ____.

3 The ____ Bridge is one of the longest suspension bridges.

B Write a sentence to answer each question.

1 Name three British suspension bridges.

2 What are the main steel cables hung between?

3 What happened to the Tacoma Narrows Bridge?

Numbers and colours can be adjectives (describing words).
Number adjectives describe the *number* of nouns.
Example: There are **two** bridges.
They can also describe the *order* of nouns.
Example: This is the **second** bridge.

Colour adjectives describe the colour of nouns.
Example: The **blue** water sparkled in the sun.

A Write the order words that go with these numbers.

number	two	one	seven	ten	three
order	second				

B Write five sentences about this picture.
Each sentence must have a colour adjective in it.

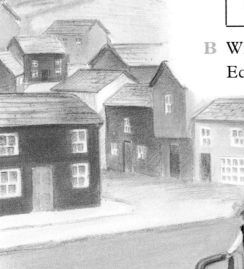

Notice what
happens to
the letter **y**.

An adjective is a 'describing' word. We use a **comparative** adjective when we compare two things.
To make a comparative adjective we add **er**, or **ier** if there is a letter **y**.
Example: This bridge is long**er** than the Severn Bridge.

We use a **superlative** adjective when we compare three or more things. To make a superlative adjective we add **est**, or **iest** if there is a letter **y**.
Examples: The Humber Bridge is the long**est** bridge in Britain. It is closed on the wind**iest** days in the year.

adjective	comparative	superlative
long	long**er**	long**est**
old	old**er**	old**est**
busy	bus**ier**	bus**iest**
windy	wind**ier**	wind**iest**

A Choose a comparative or superlative adjective from the tinted box above for these sentences.

1 The Forth Railway Bridge is o____ than the Forth Road Bridge.

2 The traffic on the bridge is b____ during the rush hour.

3 The Humber Bridge is the l____ suspension bridge in Britain.

4 The o____ bridges were made from a log or a slab of stone.

B Copy and complete the table below.

adjective	comparative	superlative
long	longer	longest
slow	____	____
high	____	____
happy	____	____
small	____	____
pretty	____	____

Remember, **adverbs** describe verbs. They tell *how*, *when* or *where* something happened. Many adverbs end in **ly**.
Examples:
The bridge swayed **dangerously**. (*how?*)
The bridge collapsed **today**. (*when?*)
The bridge stood **here**. (*where?*)

A The words in the box are adverbs. Sort them into lists depending on whether they tell us *how*, *when*, or *where* something happened. Like this:

how	**when**	**where**
dangerously	today	here

carefully	helpfully	inside	tomorrow	early
here	far	happily	later	now
then	out	kindly	everywhere	quickly

SPELLING

'oa' pattern

A Write down the **oa** words you can find in this picture.

QUIZ

Bridge builders

Build a bridge with six logs. Each log must have a word. Each word must begin with the last two letters of the log in front. Like this:

flat   ice   reach
attic   centre   chin

Aztec writing

The Aztecs lived in Mexico about five hundred years ago. They did not have an alphabet but wrote in pictures, called 'glyphs'. Some glyphs were pictures of objects to give the idea of an action, like 'war' or 'travel'. Some words were difficult to draw, so they drew glyphs of the sounds of the word. They were not exact, but everyone knew what they meant.

Their city of Quauhtitlan was written like this:

The first part of the name of the city was **Quauh** which is close to the sound for 'tree' (**quauitl**):

The last part of the name of the city was **titlan** which is close to the sound for 'teeth' (**tlantli**):

 =  +

The Aztecs also wrote numbers using glyphs.

1 to 19 were shown by fingers:

20 was shown by a flag:

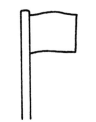

400 was shown by a feather:

COMPREHENSION

A Copy these sentences. Fill in the missing words or numbers.

1 The ____ did not have an alphabet.

2 They wrote in pictures which were called ____.

3 This glyph ∩∩∩ shows number ____.

B Write a sentence to answer each question.

1 What is a glyph?

2 How did the Aztecs write Quauhtitlan?

3 How might they have written 420?

VOCABULARY

Words and pictures

A Make your own glyphs for these words.

1 dog   2 cup   3 rain

4 ball   5 butter   6 coat

Compound words

Only draw one buttercup in the last glyph.

A Make glyphs for these compound words. Remember, compound words are two smaller words joined together.

1 cupboard ☕ + 📕 = cupboard

2 raincoat   3 armchair

4 three hotdogs   5 20 buttercups

> A noun is a name of a person, place or thing.
> Special names are called **proper nouns**.
> The first letter of a **proper noun** is always a capital letter.
> *Examples:* Quauhtitlan, Aztecs, Tracey, Manchester

A Copy these words. Put a tick by the nouns.

girl   Aztec   running   tree   was   Helen

Remember to start each sentence with a capital letter.

B Write these sentences correctly.
Give a capital letter to each proper noun.

1 the aztecs lived in mexico

2 kevin and katie have made a model aztec temple

3 janu and michaela went to the museum in aberdeen

SPELLING

Singular and plural nouns

Adding 's'

> 'Glyph' is **singular**. We mean only one glyph.
> 'Glyphs' is **plural**. We mean more than one glyph.
> We add **s** to show that we mean more than one.

A Copy this table. Write the plurals for these nouns.

singular	glyph	sound	number	finger
plural	glyphs			

's', 'x', 'ch' and 'sh' endings

A We need to add **es** to some nouns to make them plural.
These nouns all end with **s, x, ch** or **sh**.
Copy this table. Write the plurals for these nouns.

singular	bus	bush	six	tax	arch	church
plural						

B Add **s** or **es** to each of these words to make them plural.

stream   field   wish   glass   fox   torch
span   match   cart   step   rock   grass

Dictionary guide words

ABCDEFGHIJKLMNOPQRSTUVWXYZ

At the top of each page of a dictionary there are two words. These words are the first and last words on the page. Every word listed on the page comes between these guide words.

Example: adverb – allow

A On which dictionary pages would you find these words?

| adverb – allow | nut – only | putty – railings |

1 oblong = nut – only

2 onion   3 puzzle   4 aircraft

5 oil   6 rabbit   7 quack

8 alligator   9 radish   10 nylon

B Look at these pairs of guide words.

Which of the words in the box would be on each page?

| brave   flee   lucky   piano   raspberry   usual   sniff |

1 photo – plaice = piano

2 finch – flung   3 loch – mackerel

4 unit – vanilla   5 bracelet – budgerigar

6 railway – recorder   7 slide – snout

Exploring the rock pool

crab

shrimps

We explore the rock pool,
A small world of its own:
The scuttling crab, quick shrimps,
Sea-polished stone
With hints of colours
Enhanced by the light –
Refracting water
Making all so bright.
The strands of seaweed
Verdant, sleek as silk,
The tiny limpets,
Shells white as milk.
A sea in miniature
Which lasts just for a day,
When the tide renews it
Washing the old away.

John Cotton

limpets

seaweed

Glossary
enhanced means improved
refracting means changing the light
verdant means fresh and green coloured

A Copy these sentences. Fill in the missing words.

1 In the pool lives a scuttling ____ and quick ____.

2 The stones are ____ by the sea.

3 The rock pool lasts for just a ____.

B Write a sentence to answer each question.

1 What creatures live in the rock pool?

2 Why does this 'sea in miniature' last for just a day?

3 Which words in the poem rhyme?

VOCABULARY

Compound words

A Take one word from each box to make a compound word. Remember, a compound word is when two other words are joined together.
Like this: tooth + ache = toothache

up	after
screw	sea
pine	thunder
home	tooth

set	ache
work	storm
noon	apple
weed	driver

Similes

Similes describe something by comparing it to something similar. They often begin with **as** or **like**.
Example: The shells were **as white as milk**.

A Copy these sentences and neatly underline the similes.

1 The clear water sparkled like diamonds.

2 The seaweed was as sleek as silk.

3 The shell was as pretty as a picture.

B Make up some of your own sentences using similes.
Like this: The children were **as quiet as mice**.

Word families

A Find the four word families in the box.

Like this: 1 explore, explorer, explored, exploring

explore	agree	explorer	quick
quicker	quickly	discover	explored
discovery	agreement	quickest	agreeable
discovered	discovering	agreed	exploring

GRAMMAR

'Active' verbs

A Copy these sentences and underline the verbs.
Remember, most verbs are active or 'doing' words.
They tell us what is being done in a sentence.

1 Explore the beach.

2 Collect different sorts of shells.

3 Wash them in the sea.

4 Make a display.

'Being' verbs

Most verbs are active or 'doing' verbs,
but verbs can also be about **'being'**. These verbs are
am, **is**, **are**, **was**, **were**, **will be**, and **to be**.
Example: The pool **is** cold.

A Use a different 'being' verb in each sentence.

1 I ____ cold.   2 We ____ happy.

3 Our teacher ____ here.   4 She ____ pleased.

5 We ____ coming to stay.   6 I want ____ famous!

B Write five sentences, each with a different 'being' verb.

'oy' and 'oi' pattern

Look
Cover
Remember
Write
Check

A Find the words in the box which are missing from these sentences.

boy	voyage	royal	coin
pointed	spoil	toy	annoy
joyful	boil	noise	voice
enjoyed	destroy	toilet	soil

1 We ____ playing in the rock pools.

2 The ship set out on its ____.

3 The boy ____ at the crab.

4 There was so much ____ that all the creatures hid.

B Make up some sentences using **oi** and **oy** words.

Plurals

'y' endings

Remember
the vowels:
a, e, i, o, u.

We need to add **ies** to some nouns to make them plural.
You will spot these nouns because they end with **y**.
Example: one stor**y**, two stor**ies**
But if the letter in front of the **y** is a vowel, simply add **s**.
Examples: to**y** toy**s**, da**y** days

A Change these words into plurals.

1 toy   2 boy   3 bay

4 valley   5 alley   6 motorway

B Now change these words into plurals.

1 day   2 jay   3 fly   4 pony

5 fairy   6 story   7 activity   8 quay

9 trolley   10 way   11 baby   12 berry

QUIZ

Which of these two lines is longer?

1 >——<   2 <——>

Which of these three lines is the longest?

1 <——>   2 >——<   3 ———

The Chinese princess

The princess gazed up sadly at the Emperor of China's Great Wall. This was where her husband had been forced to work. He had died here, in the hot sun, crushed beneath a pile of falling rocks. She had heard awful stories about the wall. Hundreds had died as they worked. The wall had been built over the bodies where they fell.

How was she ever going to find her husband's body if it was sprawled under masses of rock? She wanted to take his body away and bury it herself.

Suddenly she saw something at her side. A friendly spirit curled out of the bushes. "Princess," it said, "I have come to help you. First cut your finger and then hold it out in front of you. The drops of blood will lead to your husband." With that, the spirit vanished.

She took a thorn and pricked her finger. Drops of blood splashed down on the ground. She followed the spots to the wall. The princess was overcome with joy and sorrow. As the spirit had promised, the trail had drawn her to the body of her husband.

This Chinese legend is a very old story. The Emperor Shih Huang Ti gave orders for the building of the Great Wall of China over 2000 years ago. It was to be a huge wall to keep out all his enemies.

Adapted from *A Beautiful Legend* by Richard Worsnop

China's Great Wall fact file
Time to build: 10 years
Length: 2400 kilometres   **Height**: 10 metres
Special notes: It is said to be the only feature built on Earth which is visible from the Moon. It is described as one of the 'Seven Wonders of the World'.

COMPREHENSION

A Copy these sentences. Fill in the missing words.

1 The princess was sad because her husband was ____.

2 A ____ helped her to find his body.

3 She followed the drops of ____ from her finger.

B Write a sentence to answer each question.

1 When was the Great Wall of China built?

2 Why was it built?

3 Do you think the story of the sad princess is true?

VOCABULARY

Dictionary definitions

A Find these words in the story. Imagine you were making a dictionary, and write a definition for each one. Remember, a definition is the meaning of a word.

overcome   awful   sorrow   legend

B Now look up each word in your dictionary and write the dictionary definition. Is it similar to your definition?

Contractions

Contractions are used in place of two words.
Examples: **It's** is a contraction for **it is**.
Don't is a contraction for **do not**.
The words are made smaller by leaving out some letters and putting in an apostrophe (') in their place.

A Find the contractions in these sentences.
Next to each contraction write the words which it replaces.

1 The princess didn't know what to do.

2 "I can't bear to think of him buried there," she said.

3 They shouldn't be so cruel.

4 "I'll help you," said the spirit.

5 "I won't ever come here again," cried the princess.

PUNCTUATION

Paragraphs

A **paragraph** is a group of sentences about one main idea. To show our reader when a new **paragraph** is beginning we start a new line. A **paragraph** should have sentences about the same subject.

A Look at the story again and answer these questions.

1 How many paragraphs has the writer used?

2 Is the first paragraph a good start to the story?

3 Does the last paragraph finish the story?

4 Do all the paragraphs have the same number of sentences?

B Find a story you have written, or choose one from a book. Answer the same questions about your story or piece of writing.

Punctuation marks

SPELLING

'aw' pattern

A All the punctuation marks have been left out of these sentences. Write them correctly.

1 the legend is about a sad princess

2 shih huang ti was a cruel emperor

3 he ruled china for many years

4 i will help you said the kind spirit

5 why is the emperor so unkind she asked

The **aw** pattern can be at the beginning of a word (**aw**ful),
or in the middle of a word (spr**aw**led),
or at the end of a word (s**aw**).

A 1 Write all the **aw** words in the story.

2 Write all the **aw** words hidden in this wordsearch.
The words are across and down.

```
b z s p r a w l
w a w a y p p a
l d a q c l a w
h a w t h o r n
a w a r e q p j
w n k r a w a a
k s e e s a w w
```

3 Now make your own wordsearch with **aw** words.
Try it on a friend.

QUIZ
Missing vowels

Can you see what is missing in this sentence?
My tchr mks m wrk t hrd.
Yes, all the vowels have been left out.

Write a note to a friend leaving out the vowels.
Your friend must reply to show that it has been understood.

Check-up 2

A Copy and complete the table. Fill in the missing adjectives.

adjective	comparative	superlative
big	bigger	biggest
——	shorter	——
——	——	smallest
long	——	——
——	prettier	——
funny	——	——
——	older	——
——	——	heaviest
kind	——	——
——	——	saddest

B Choose a word from each box which can be joined together to make a compound word.

thunder	note	some	screw	every	tooth

times	ache	storm	body	driver	paper

C Copy these contractions.
Next to each write out the words in full.
Like this:

1 it's = it is   2 don't   3 we've   4 haven't

5 doesn't   6 he's   7 weren't   8 they've

D Write the contractions for these words. Like this:

1 should not = shouldn't   2 would not

3 I will   4 is not

5 they are   6 will not

7 has not   8 she is

PUNCTUATION AND GRAMMAR

A Write these sentences. Put in the missing capital letters and punctuation marks. Underline the proper nouns.

1 janu emma and steven are going to manchester

2 can i come too asked william

3 yes you can they all said

4 william asked what time will we get home

B Write five adjectives to describe this child.

C Write these sentences. Underline all the active or 'doing' verbs in red and the 'being' verbs in blue.

1 I am too cold to play any more.

2 I was told to be home early.

3 We will be shouted at!

4 Mum is probably worried about us.

SPELLING

A Write the plural of these words.

1 toy = toys	4 fly	7 jay
2 key	5 story	8 baby
3 day	6 berry	9 party

B Choose **s** or **es** to make the plural of these words.

1 cat	4 arch	7 church
2 bus	5 brush	8 fox
3 horse	6 finger	9 six

Castle siege

When an enemy surrounds a castle or town it is called a siege. Food and other supplies are cut off while the enemy attacks.

In the past, attackers would camp outside a castle. If there was a moat they would fill part of it in. They could then get close to the walls and try to climb over using ropes and ladders.

Sometimes the attackers would break down the castle gates with a battering ram. They would also try to get into the castle by digging a tunnel under the walls. They would even build huge catapults to hurl giant rocks at the walls to break them down.

While this was happening, the defenders inside the castle would shoot arrows through slits in the walls. They would also throw boiling tar or heavy objects down on the attackers. Sometimes at night they would send out small raiding parties through hidden gates in the castle walls, to take the attackers by surprise.

COMPREHENSION

A Copy these sentences. Fill in the missing words.

1 When an enemy surrounded a castle it was called a ____.

2 First they would stop all ____ getting inside the castle.

3 A ____ ____ was used to break down the gate.

B Write a sentence to answer each question.

1 How did the attacking army try to climb the walls?

2 What were the catapults used for?

3 What methods did the people inside the castle use to defend themselves?

VOCABULARY

Questions

A question word at the beginning of a sentence must have a capital letter.

> **Questions** often begin with one of these question words:
> **when   what   why   where**
> **will   how   who   which**
> Question sentences always end with a question mark (**?**).

A Use a question word to complete these sentences.

1 ____ did the soldiers attack the castle?

2 ____ weapons did they use?

3 ____ the defenders surrender?

4 ____ did they shoot their arrows?

B Make up questions to go with these answers.
The first is done for you.

1 The castle is in Ireland. Where is the castle?

2 There were one hundred soldiers attacking the castle.

3 Tar and rocks were thrown at the attackers.

4 The soldiers fired arrows through slits in the walls.

GRAMMAR

Possessive nouns

> To show that something belongs to someone or something we use an apostrophe (') and an **s**, like this: **'s**.
> *Example:* the knight**'s** castle
> (the castle belonging to the knight)
> **Knight's** is called a **possessive noun**.

A Write these in a shorter way. Use a possessive noun. The first one is done for you.

1 The castle belonging to the knight. = the knight's castle

2 The cottage belonging to the peasant.

3 The bow belonging to the archer.

4 The horse belonging to the soldier.

5 The hat the girl is wearing.

6 The shoes the boy is wearing.

7 The sword the knight is using.

8 The shield the soldier is carrying.

SPELLING

'igh' pattern

Look
Cover
Remember
Write
Check

A Copy these sentences. Fill in the missing **igh** words. The words below will help you.

knight	night	flight	height		
light	fight	high	bright	fright	might
lighter	fighter	higher	brighter	frighten	mighty
lightest	fighting	highest	brightest	frightening	

1 The ____ rode into battle.

2 We had to stop the dogs ____.

3 It was ____ when they attacked the castle.

4 The walls were too ____ to climb.

5 We could see by the ____ of the moon.

B Copy the words in the box above. Try to learn them.

A Here are some word pairs.

They are homophones because they sound the same.

One word in each pair has a silent **k**.

knight	knot	know	knew
night	not	no	new

Put each pair of words in a short sentence.

The first one is done for you.

1 The **knight** was scared of the dark **night**.

QUIZ

Vowel wordsquares

> The five vowel letters in the alphabet are:
>
>   a e i o u
>
> Almost all words have a vowel in them, so vowels
> are important.

Each of these wordsquares has a different missing vowel.

The same vowel is used in each of its empty spaces.

Solve the wordsquares.

1

h		t
	■	
m		g

2

r		t
	■	
m		p

3

h		t
	■	
p		n

4

h		p
	■	
t		p

5

w		t
	■	
d		n

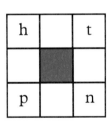

Mary, Queen of Scots

Mary became Queen of Scotland when her father died. She was only six days old.

When she was six years old, she was sent to live with King Henry of France. When she was sixteen, she married his eldest son Francis. Shortly afterwards, Francis and Mary became King and Queen of France. Some people thought that Mary should also have been the Queen of England instead of Queen Elizabeth I.

After Francis died, Mary came back to Scotland. Although she was still young, she had been away for some years. She cried when some people said that they did not want her to be Queen of Scotland any more. A few years later, she married Henry Darnley. When Henry was murdered, some people said that Mary had paid a killer to get rid of him. Other people said that an earl called Bothwell had done it. Mary became very unpopular. So when Mary and Bothwell got married, soldiers attacked their castle and took them prisoner.

Mary was forced to sign a piece of paper saying that her baby son James was now King of Scotland. She was locked up in a castle on an island, but a boy who lived in the castle felt sorry for her. He made holes in all the boats on the island, except one. He then took Mary to the only good boat and she escaped to England.

Mary went to Queen Elizabeth I for help, but Elizabeth was suspicious of Mary. She knew that some people wanted Mary to be Queen of England instead. So Elizabeth kept Mary as a prisoner and in the end put her to death.

Later, when Queen Elizabeth I died, Mary's son James became King of England as well as Scotland.

COMPREHENSION

A Copy these sentences. Fill in the missing words.

1 Mary became Queen of Scotland at ____ days old.

2 Mary's first husband was ____.

3 Mary's son became King of ____ as well as Scotland.

B Write a sentence to answer each question.

1 Who did some people think murdered Henry Darnley?

2 Why was Elizabeth suspicious of Mary?

3 How did Mary escape from the island?

Bought and **brought** often get confused.
Bought has to do with **b**uying something.
Brought has to do with **br**inging something.

Remember
the **r** in
b**r**ought
and b**r**ing.

A Write these sentences and add **bought** or **brought**.

1 The little princess was ____ to live with King Henry.

2 He ____ her fine clothes to wear.

3 Prince Francis spent a lot of money and ____ a beautiful ring.

4 Mary was ____ back to Scotland in a fine coach.

5 They ____ her the papers to sign.

In every sentence there is a **verb**.
Every **verb** has a **subject**.
The **subject** is the main person or thing which is related to the **verb**.
Example: **Mary escaped** on horseback.
          subject   verb

A Copy each of these sentences.
Draw a neat circle round the verb.
Then draw a line under the subject.
The first one is done to help you.

1 <u>Mary</u> (lived) in France.

2 Mary married Henry Darnley.

3 The soldiers captured Mary and Bothwell.

4 A boy lived in the castle.

5 Elizabeth imprisoned Mary in Fotheringay Castle.

B Write these sentences.

Choose one of the words in brackets to fill the gaps.

1 The subject of the sentence is usually at the ____ of the
   sentence. (end, beginning)

2 The verb usually comes ____ the subject. (before, after)

3 The subject is usually a ____. (noun, verb, adjective)

4 The subject of the sentence is the ____ person or thing
   which is related to the verb. (main, last)

C Copy four sentences from a reading book.
Circle the verbs and underline the subjects.

Your answers
to Part A
will help you.

SPELLING

'ea' pattern

sea

treasure

The **ea** pattern can make two different sounds.
Examples: Mary crossed the s**ea**.
She took her tr**ea**sure.

A Sort the **ea** words in the box into two groups.

1 Words with an **ea** sound as in tr**ea**sure.
2 Words with an **ea** sound as in s**ea**.

death	beach	feather	heavy	clean
teacher	leap	peace	head	ready
weather	deaf	treasure	mean	stream

B Try to find some more **ea** words to add to each list.

QUIZ

Royal riddle

My first letter is in 'quack' but not in 'rack'.
My second is in 'put' but not in 'pot'.
My third is in 'ten' but not in 'tan'.
My fourth is in 'then' but not in 'than'.
My last letter is in 'one' but not in 'two'.

What am I?

School in Stuart times

In Stuart times, parents had to pay if they wanted their children to go to school. Not many parents had enough money to spare, but they knew that if their children didn't learn to read and write they would not get good jobs when they grew up. This letter was written in 1647.

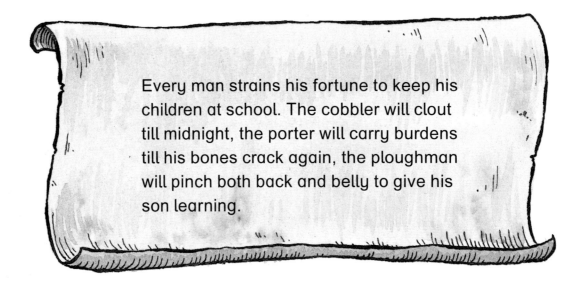

Every man strains his fortune to keep his children at school. The cobbler will clout till midnight, the porter will carry burdens till his bones crack again, the ploughman will pinch both back and belly to give his son learning.

Most adults could not read or write or even sign their names. On this document only four people were able to sign their names, the others had to put their mark.

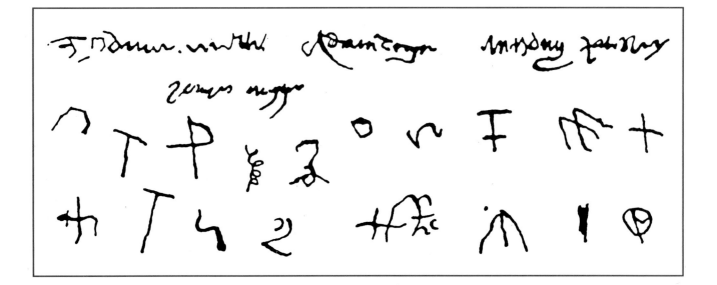

Most children didn't go to school. Here is what a child, lucky enough to go to school, might have written in a diary at the time.

It was cold and dark as I walked to school with Alfred this morning. Lessons started at 6 o'clock. Far too early to be trying to learn Latin, writing and arithmetic, I reckon! Our teacher read out the Latin words and we had to chant them back. It was very boring.

Poor Alfred got beaten again because he can't remember how to do division sums. I don't see how that will help him remember. I said I would try to help him.

COMPREHENSION

A Copy these sentences. Fill in the missing words.

1 Most people could not _____ or write.

2 People who could not sign their name put their ____.

3 Lessons started at ____ o'clock in the morning.

B Write a sentence to answer each question.

1 Why did parents work hard to pay for their children to go to school?

2 What were the main lessons taught in schools?

3 What made the lessons so boring?

> **Gender words** tell us whether a person or animal is female or male.
>
> *Example:* A **girl** is a female child. A **boy** is a male child.

A Copy and complete this table of females and males.

female	male
girl	boy
——	father
aunt	——
grandmother	——
cow	——
——	ram
——	brother
——	king

B Sort the words below into females and males.

> daughter tiger waitress grandma headmaster son
> actress bridegroom prince actor aunt princess
> waiter tigress uncle headmistress bride grandad

> We use a **full stop** (.) at the end of a sentence. We use them most of the time. We use a **question mark** (?) when a question is asked. We use an **exclamation mark** (!) when someone is hurt, cross or surprised, or something happens suddenly.

School starts at six o'clock**.**

School starts at six o'clock**?**

School starts at six o'clock**!**

? and !
have a full stop
built in.

A Write these short sentences and add the correct punctuation mark at the end of each one.

1 Come here this minute

2 Will you be at school

3 Go away at once

4 What's your name

5 The girls stayed at home

6 Quick, she's coming

7 Ouch, that hurt

8 Can you help me

SPELLING

'ough' pattern

A The **ough** pattern can stand for several different sounds.

1 Read these words. Which **ough** letters sound the same?

trough	though	bough	thorough
rough	bought	plough	cough
tough	dough	borough	through	brought

2 Which word in the box is the odd-one-out?

QUIZ

Odd-one-out

Find the odd-one-out in these lists.

1 pencil pen biro apple

2 doctor table teacher soldier

3 horse cow sheep pig snake

4 car lorry bicycle bus

Make up some odd-one-out lists to try on your friends.

Living things breathe

All animals must have air to live. Air is a mixture of many gases. The most important gas for breathing is oxygen.

We breathe air through our noses. It goes down a tube, called the windpipe, into our lungs. Our lungs are two large, spongy bags in our chest. We can see our chests get bigger as we breathe air in.

Our lungs help oxygen in the air to get into our blood. The oxygen then goes with the blood to all parts of our body. People going to places where there may not be enough oxygen must take it with them in tanks.

Most big animals get oxygen through their lungs as well, but some small animals breathe in other ways.

Earthworms take in oxygen through their thin skin. Slugs and snails have a large hole in their sides and insects have many tiny holes to breathe through.

Water creatures have other ways of breathing. A water beetle comes to the surface and puts the tip of its tail out into the air. It then takes a bubble of air under the water. It breathes the air in the bubble through little tubes in its tail.

Fishes get their oxygen from air which is in the water. A fish uses its gills to take oxygen out of the water. You can see the air in water, when water is heated in a saucepan and it bubbles.

COMPREHENSION

A Copy these sentences. Fill in the missing words.

1 The most important gas we breathe is ____.

2 We breathe air through our ____.

3 Insects breathe through tiny ____ in their sides.

B Write a sentence to answer each question.

1 How is the oxygen passed around our body?

2 How do slugs breathe?

3 How can we see that there is air in water?

VOCABULARY

Synonyms

Words that mean the same, or nearly the same, are called **synonyms**.
Examples: large, big   strong, powerful

A Find the synonyms in the box.

tiny	enough	small	under	maybe	heat
break	shout	perhaps	warm	beneath	
get	obtain	sufficient	yell	smash	

B Write a sentence for three of the synonyms you have found to show they mean the same. Like this:

1 We (**obtain/get**) oxygen from the air.

Words such as **The firefighter said**, or **I shouted**, tell us who is speaking. These words may come before, in the middle of, or at the end of the words actually spoken.

If the spoken words are separated, we don't need a capital letter for the second part. This is because it is still part of the same sentence.

Examples:

The firefighter said, "This smoke is so thick it is hard to breathe."

"This smoke is so thick," **the firefighter said**, "it is hard to breathe."

"This smoke is so thick it is hard to breathe," **said the firefighter**.

A Copy the words that are actually spoken in these sentences.

1 The air, panted the climber, is very thin up here.

2 Please help, cried the woman, he is not breathing properly!

3 Swimming underwater, said the diver, is an amazing thing to do.

4 All I hope, said the astronaut, is that this spacesuit doesn't leak.

B Now write the whole of these sentences, putting in inverted commas.

GRAMMAR

Subjects and
predicates

All sentences
begin with
a capital letter
and end with
a full stop.

A simple sentence has two parts.

The **subject** is the thing or person written about.

The **predicate** is the rest of the sentence.

It includes the verb, and it tells us what is happening.

Example: A water beetle breathes through its tail.

        subject   *predicate*

A Make simple sentences from these subjects and predicates.

subject	predicate
Fishes	have two lungs.
Earthworms	have a shell.
Humans	breathe through their skin.
Snails	breathe through gills.

B Copy these sentences. Then divide them into subjects and predicates. Draw a neat line under the verbs. Like this:

1 Earthworms / <u>take</u> in oxygen through their skin.

2 Snails collect air through their sides.

3 Astronauts carry oxygen tanks on spacewalks.

4 Humans breathe air through their noses.

5 The water beetle collects an air bubble.

SPELLING

'o' sound

Look
Cover
Remember
Write
Check

The letter **o** sometimes sounds like the letter **u** in 'b**u**t'.

A Choose two of these groups of words and write them out carefully. Now learn them.

other	love glove	London won	someone
mother	shove	wonder	come month
brother	lovely	Monday	coming
another	cover oven	son done	monkey
nothing	above	honey	money

B Make up a sentence with some 'o-which-sound-like-u-words'.

Mother Teresa of Calcutta

Have you ever wondered what it would be like to be famous? Some people dream that one day they will be great swimmers, footballers or athletes. Others have hopes of becoming rich musicians or film stars, and some people would even like to be Prime Minister. Every now and then, someone becomes famous just for helping other people. One famous person like this is Mother Teresa.

Mother Teresa came from Albania, a very poor country, and went to India as a Roman Catholic nun. Although some people in India are rich, she realised that many still live in terrible poverty. This made her sad and she knew she must try to help, so she started a group of nuns called the Missionaries of Charity.

Mother Teresa and the nuns who help her have now opened over fifty homes for orphan children, and in many other places they feed and care for the very poor who are too old or too sick to help themselves. They are opening more homes whenever they can.

A Copy these sentences. Fill in the missing words.

1 Mother Teresa came from ____.

2 She went to ____.

3 She was very upset to see so many ____ people.

B Write a sentence to answer each question.

1 What is Mother Teresa's organisation called?

2 What does it try to do?

3 If you could be famous, what would you like to be known for?

Abbreviations are short forms of words.
Example: Nuns are often called 'Sisters'. If you were to write to a nun you would write **Sr** in front of her name on the envelope. **Sr** is an abbreviation for Sister.

A Write these lists in your book. Use a ruler to draw lines to link each abbreviation with its meaning.

abbreviation	meaning
Sr	minute
Mr	kilometre
km	Prime Minister
Rd	Road
Dr	Sister
m	Doctor
min	Mister
PM	metre
UN	United Kingdom
St	United Nations
UK	Street
RC	Roman Catholic

A **suffix** is a word ending. The suffix **ed** tells us an action has happened in the past. The suffix **ing** tells an action is happening now, in the present time.
Examples: open, open**ed,** open**ing**
help, help**ed,** help**ing**

A 1 Add **ed** suffixes to these verbs:
walk, jump, watch, shout, talk

2 Now add **ing** suffixes to the same verbs.

B 1 Write a sentence which has a word with an **ed** suffix, to show something has happened in the past.

2 Write a sentence which has a word with an **ing** suffix, to show something is happening now, in the present time.

C Copy all the words in the passage about Mother Teresa which have an ed or an **ing** suffix.

A The **er** pattern usually comes at the end of a word.
Look carefully at these words. Now cover them.
Ask a friend to check how many you can spell correctly.
Try again if you get some wrong.

mother	river	under	letter
father	water	over	pattern
brother	silver	ever	person
sister	finger	after	

Look
Cover
Remember
Write
Check

Adding 'er'

We usually double the last letter if the one before it is a single vowel (a, e, i, o, u).

The **er** letter pattern is sometimes added to words to make a new word, such as 'bigger'.
Do you see what else has happened?
Often when we add **er** to a small word we must double the last letter before adding **er**.

B Copy and complete this table.

big	bigger
swim	_____
mad	madder
win	_____
sad	_____
fit	fitter
hot	_____
run	runner

'er', 'ir', 'ur' patterns

A Use **er**, **ir** or **ur** to make each group of letters into a word.
Check your words in a dictionary.

1 oth___   2 b___nt   3 b___d   4 wat___

5 t___n   6 riv___   7 f___st   8 g___l

9 n___se   10 ch___ch   11 b___glar   12 d___ty

13 und___   14 nev___   15 Sat___day

QUIZ

About yourself

Write the letters of your name down the side of a page.
Think of phrases beginning with each letter to describe your favourite things. You might think of some serious ones and then some funny ones. Here is what Matthew chose.

My Mum's smile
Aunty Tina's jokes
TV
Teacher – sometimes!
Having fun at playtime
Eating burgers
Watching Liverpool win!

Check-up 3

VOCABULARY

A Write these sentences.
Choose the correct word in brackets to fill the gap.

1 We ____ sweets with our pocket money. (bought/brought)

2 I ____ my new trainers to school. (bought/brought)

3 My uncle ____ a present in the shop. (bought/brought)

B Copy this table. Fill in the missing words.

male	man	____	king	____	bull
female	woman	sister	____	princess	____

PUNCTUATION

A Copy this passage.
Add all the capital letters and punctuation marks.

can i stay up late tonight said brian no replied his father brian was cross why not he asked we are going to blackpool with jane ali and uncle joe tomorrow and you need to get up early in the morning said dad

GRAMMAR

A Copy these sentences. Underline the subject and circle the verb in each one.

1 Nadim walked to school.

2 The rain fell on the children.

3 The children hung their coats on the pegs.

SPELLING

A Copy this table. Fill in the missing words.

swim	swimming	swimmer
run	____	____
____	____	winner
jump	____	____
row	____	____